ERIC BAUMGARTNER'S

JAZZ IT·UP!

SERIES

MID-INTERMEDIATE PIANO SOLO

STANDARDS

T0088319

PLAYBACK+

Speed · Pitch · Balance · Loop

To access audio, visit:
www.halleonard.com/mylibrary

3386-2666-5445-8739

ISBN 978-1-4584-0239-4

WILLIS MUSIC

EXCLUSIVELY DISTRIBUTED BY

HAL•LEONARD®

7777 W. BLUEMOUND RD. P.O. BOX 13819
MILWAUKEE, WISCONSIN 53213

Visit Hal Leonard Online at
www.halleonard.com

FROM THE ARRANGER

This collection contains some of my favorite jazz standards. Now for a tune to be considered a "standard," it's got to be pretty special—more special than just a "hit"; special enough to stand the test of time. Many hit songs fade from memory not long after their initial success. By contrast, a song worthy of standard status will outlast a quick burst of fame, continue to grow in popularity and become part of our musical heritage. The songs in the following pages have done just that.

Jazz musicians love to perform these standards. Not only because they are well known, but also because the melody, harmony and lyrics (when applicable) are strong enough to withstand reinvention. Jazzers are not content to merely imitate previous versions of a tune: they look to add something unique with each performance. The result may bring out fresh aspects of the song that were less obvious in those previous versions. I've enjoyed adding a few new twists here and there to these beloved tunes but, since many of you may be new to performing jazz, for the most part I've chosen to be rather faithful to the most iconic versions.

Original publication dates for the compositions in this collection range from the late 1920s to the early 1960s. These are the years when jazz was at its peak in popularity. Represented are songs closely associated with some of the biggest names in jazz; names like Fats Waller, Duke Ellington, Dave Brubeck, Billie Holliday and Antonio Carlos Jobim. It has been a treat for me to revisit these wonderful tunes, to celebrate these wonderful composers, and to honor these standard bearers with modern arrangements.

Enjoy!

Eric Baumgartner

CONTENTS

Ain't Misbehavin'

Words by Andy Razaf
Music by Thomas "Fats" Waller and Harry Brooks
Arranged by Eric Baumgartner

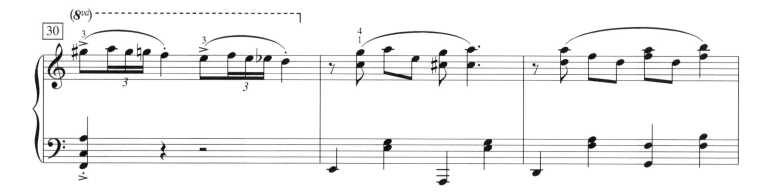

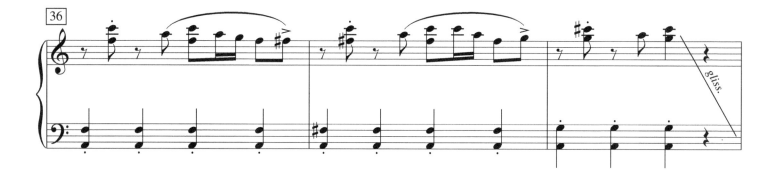

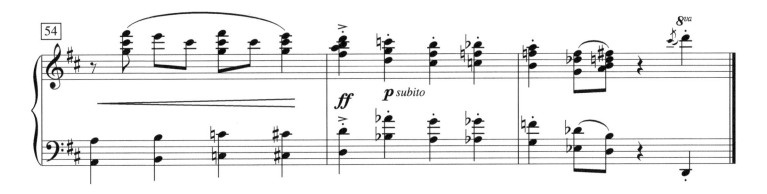

Autumn Leaves

English lyric by Johnny Mercer
French lyric by Jacques Prevert
Music by Joseph Kosma
Arranged by Eric Baumgartner

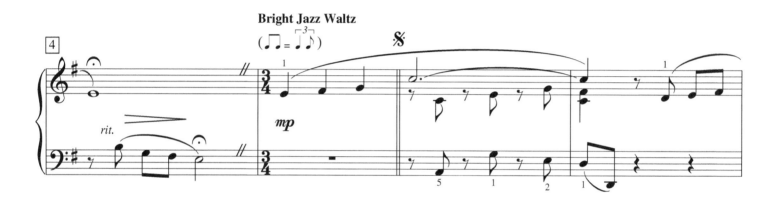

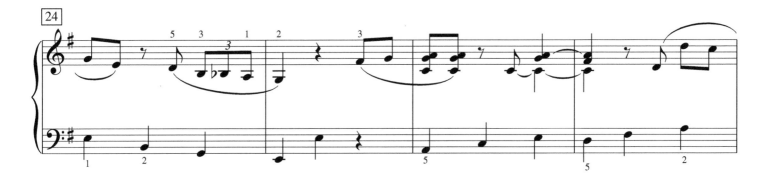

To Coda

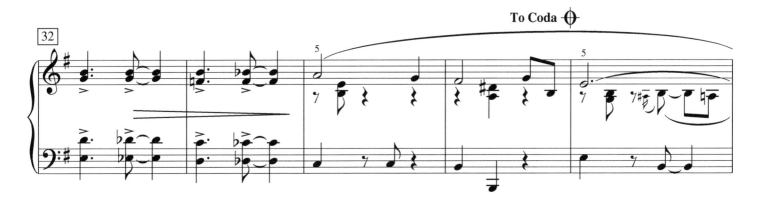

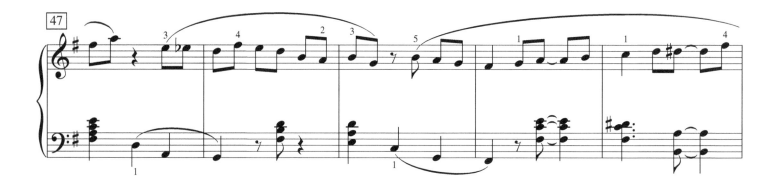

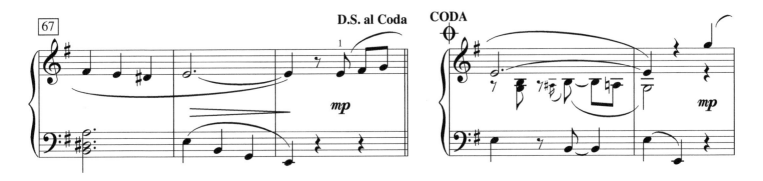

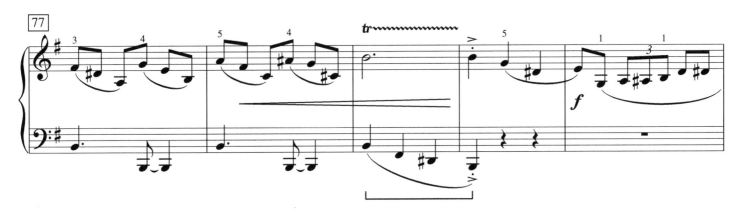

Don't Get Around Much Anymore

from SOPHISTICATED LADY

Words and Music by Duke Ellington
and Bob Russell
Arranged by Eric Baumgartner

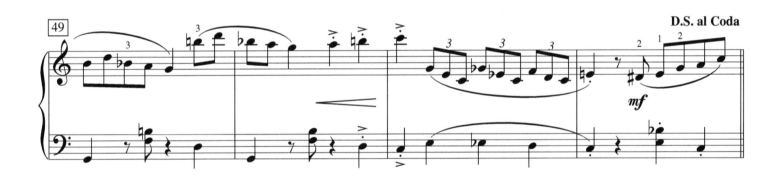

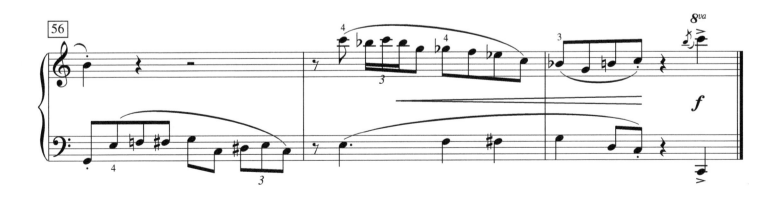

God Bless' the Child

featured in the Motion Picture LADY SINGS THE BLUES

Words and Music by Arthur Herzog Jr.
and Billie Holiday
Arranged by Eric Baumgartner

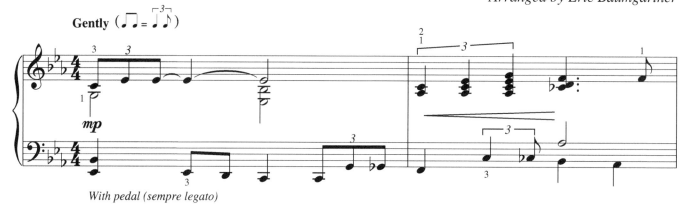

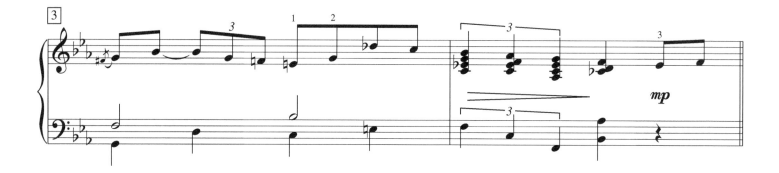

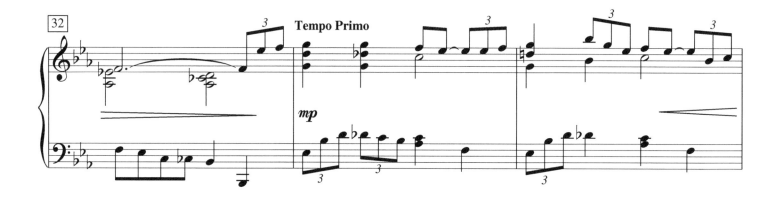

Even 8ths (no swing)

One Note Samba
(Samba de uma nota só)

Original Lyrics by Newton Mendonça
English Lyrics by Antonio Carlos Jobim
Music by Antonio Carlos Jobim
Arranged by Eric Baumgartner

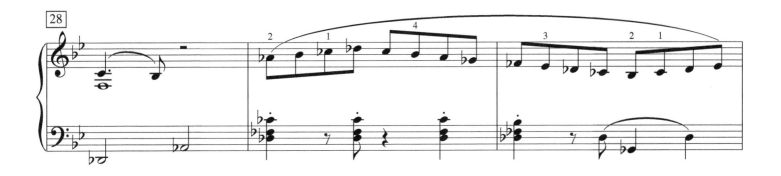

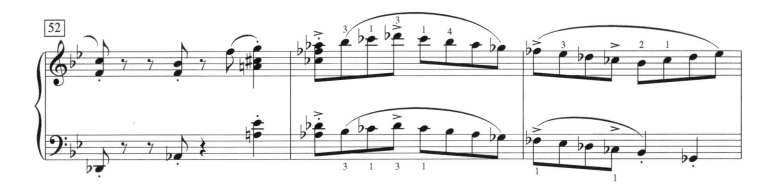

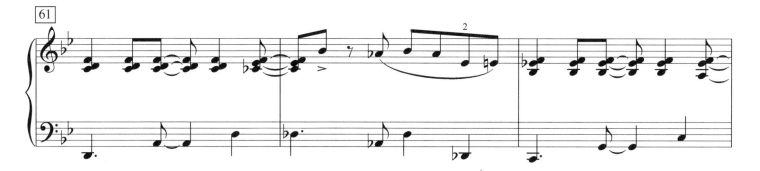

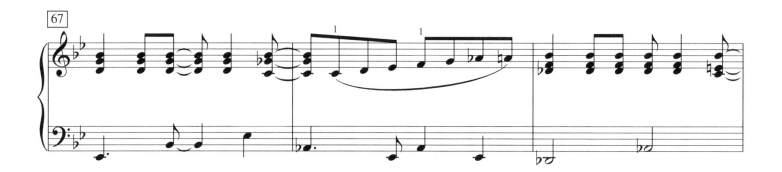

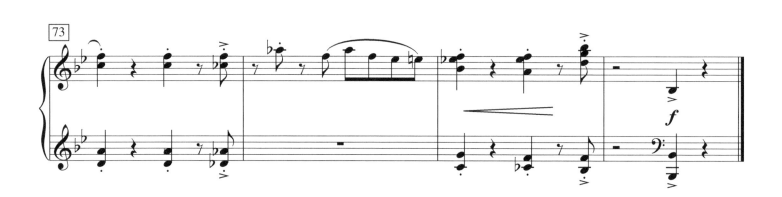

Stormy Weather

from COTTON CLUB PARADE OF 1933

Lyric by Ted Koehler
Music by Harold Arlen
Arranged by Eric Baumgartner

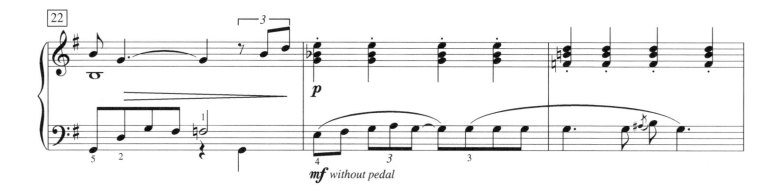

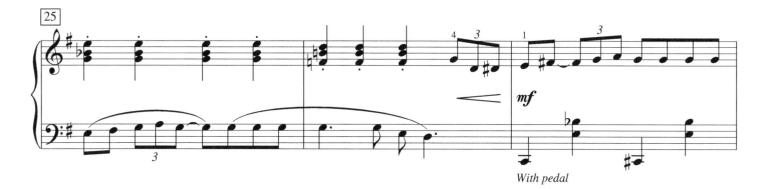

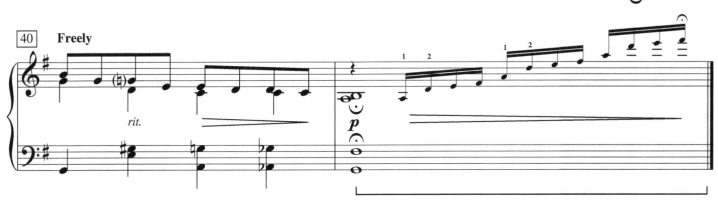

Take Five

By Paul Desmond
Arranged by Eric Baumgartner

Moderate Swing

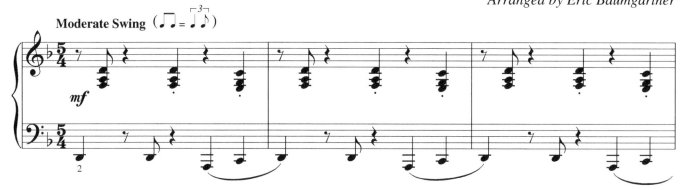

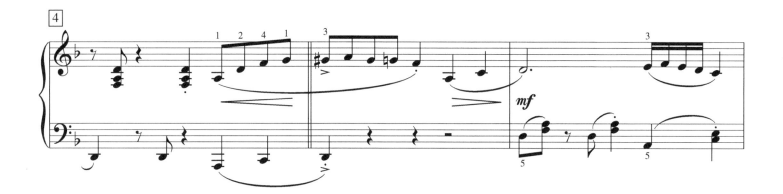

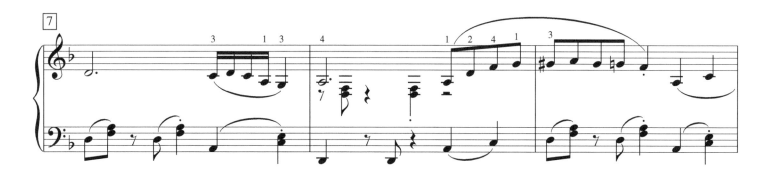

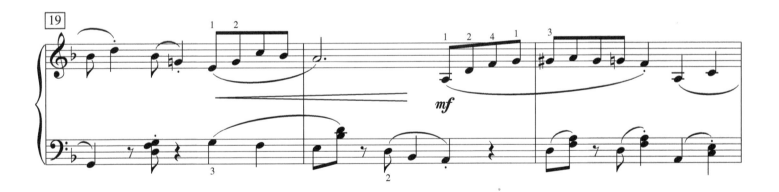

To Coda ⊕

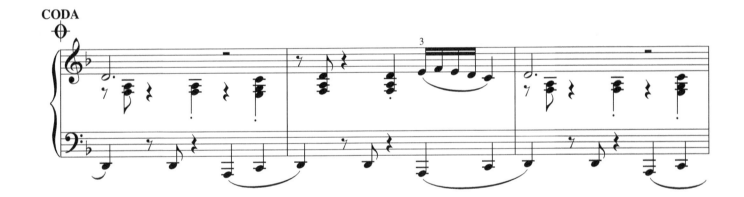

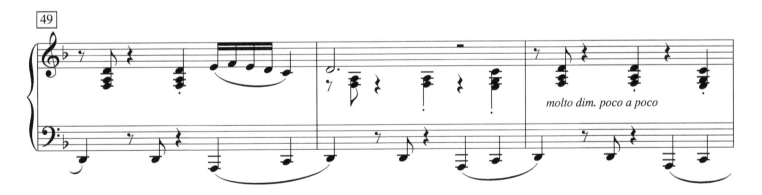

ERIC BAUMGARTNER'S JAZZ IT·UP! SERIES

Eric Baumgartner's *Jazz It Up! Series* are jazz arrangements of well-known tunes that both experienced and beginning jazz pianists will enjoy. The stylized pieces are intentionally written without chord symbols or improvisation sections, although pianists are encouraged to experiment and explore!

Christmas
TWELVE CAROLS
Mid-Intermediate Level
Deck the Hall • God Rest Ye Merry, Gentlemen • O Christmas Tree • The Coventry Carol • Good King Wenceslas • Jingle Bells, and more!

00349037 Book/Audio . $12.99

Familiar Favorites
SEVEN FOLK SONGS
Mid-Intermediate Level
All Through the Night • The Erie Canal • Greensleeves • La Cucaracha • Londonderry Air • Scarborough Fair • When the Saints Go Marching In.

00416778 Book/Audio ... $9.95

Classics
SIX CLASSICAL FAVES
Mid-Intermediate Level
Funeral March of a Marionette (Gounod) • Habanera (Bizet) • Nutcracker Rock (Tchaikovsky) • Song for the New World (Dvořák) • Spinning Song (Ellmenreich) • Symphonic Swing (Mozart).

00416867 Book/Audio ... $9.99

Standards
SEVEN FAVORITE CLASSICS
Mid-Intermediate Level
Ain't Misbehavin' • Autumn Leaves • Don't Get Around Much Anymore • God Bless' the Child • One Note Samba • Stormy Weather • Take Five.

00416903 Book/Audio . $14.99

CLOSER LOOK
View sample pages and hear audio excerpts online at www.halleonard.com

WILLIS MUSIC

EXCLUSIVELY DISTRIBUTED BY

HAL•LEONARD®

Prices, contents, and availability subject to change without notice.